DEVOURING Shakespeare

-Five Simple Tools-

Ehren Ziegler

Devouring Shakespeare: Five Simple Tools.
A Chop Bard™ Guide

Copyright © 2011 by Ehren Ziegler

All Rights Reserved. Published in the United States of America. No part of this book may be used or reproduced in any manner whatsoever without the written permission of the author.

Cover illustration and design by Shannon Sneedse
Copyright © 2008-2011 by Shannon Sneedse

Acknowledgments

To Shannon for your unfailing support & many contributions

To Kymberly for your brilliant talent

To Judy and Jerry (Mom and Dad) for everything

I thank you. I am not of many words, but I thank you.
– Much Ado About Nothing, I.i

"I don't want to make praise sound as mockery by blaring too loud the trumpets of praise, but this guide should reside, heavily dog-eared, on the desk of every teacher whose students are reticent to believe that Shakespeare is both understandable and worth their time. This simple guidebook shows good reason why Shakespeare can and should be enjoyed and studied — 400 years after he shuffled off this mortal coil.

With the plays, we must always be open to being surprised by new discoveries and we must actively seek those discoveries. This helps like a GPS. We, today, are the audience Bill W. was writing for and these pages equal one hot ticket to some of the best seats in the house."

G.Robin Smith,
Creator: The VLA-Shakespeare Project
"To Each Their Own", a V-Act Elizabethan Comedy
Author of the forthcoming "The Five Same Characters found in every Shakespeare Play" – "The DOLTS"

"Ehren Ziegler, master of all things Shakespeare, has done it again. As if producing Chop Bard podcast wasn't enough to save the masses from misunderstanding Will, Ziegler has now written a handy little guide that all of us (not just teachers) can use to aid our ability to enjoy plays that have more than stood the test of time. Pick up this little volume and pour it onto the porches of your ears. Feel the calm suffuse your soul as you realize--once and for all--that understanding and enjoying Shakespeare is easy (for you or your students) and that a brave new world of literary love has opened before you."

Heather Ordover,
Editrix, "What Would Madame Defarge Knit?"
Host of the CraftLit podcast.

Contents

Acknowledgments	iii
Authors Note	1
What we intend	3
Who's it for?	3
The Guidelines	4
The One Rule	6
I	10
II	18
III	24
IV	30
V	36
Conclusion	40
Time Line	42
References	44

Author's Note

In June 2008, I started the Chop Bard podcast to share my passion for the plays of William Shakespeare and spread the word that his plays are not only relevant to our times but also immensely entertaining.

Shakespeare is hardly short on respect, yet some people continue to believe that his work is highbrow and boring. Thus was born the show's motto (and goal): *The cure for boring Shakespeare.*

It quickly became evident that the first challenge when attempting to understand Shakespeare is where to begin. There is an abundance of critical and enlightening resources, but which ones should you use first? For a beginner, choosing where to invest their attention can be a daunting task; for an expert, sharing their knowledge can be a chore to organize.

A further complication is the multitude of approaches to Shakespeare. While very little is actually required to enjoy Shakespeare, it is generally agreed that an understanding of his words, use of verse, and place in history, along with the many theatre techniques used to stage his plays, is essential for analyzing his work. With so many elements, it's difficult to decide which ones to commit to first—on its own, each could lead to lifelong study. In addition, theater is a living art form in a constant state of evolution, so the relationship of Shakespeare to current theatre practice is always changing. It's very easy to feel overwhelmed by the sheer volume of work about Shakespeare before you even get to the first line of an actual play.

I thought, somewhere in all this mess, we need common points of reference strong enough to bind all the plays, enrich our experience, and give us tools on which we can always rely. So, I sat down and drew some guidelines based on my own experience and encounters with Shakespeare in hopes of discovering those reference points. I offer the result: simple tools for devouring Shakespeare.

Ehren Ziegler
January 24, 2011

What we intend

The purpose of this guide is to equip the reader with a common language for understanding Shakespeare. By keeping our method simple and our guidebook small, we hope the reader will quickly grasp this language and move on quickly to the important stuff—enjoying the plays.

My personal goal is to kick the "stuffiness" out of Shakespeare—make him more accessible without dumbing him down. Shakespeare's words and writing style may seem alien to our contemporary sensibilities, but the stories and ideas contained in his plays are as recognizable and as universal as comfort food and loud neighbors. If you look beyond the highbrow nonsense you'll see that Shakespeare is writing about all of us.

Who's it for?

This guide is for anyone and everyone who interacts with Shakespeare. If you are a novice, it will offer an unintimidating means to ease into a complex world. If you've had some experience with the Bard, this guide can help you dig deeper. Perhaps you are a master of all things Shakespeare. This guide may well serve to strip away some of the detritus accumulated from your many years of study, reminding you to look again with fresh eyes at the simple wonders of these plays.

The Guidelines

Simple tools for a daunting task.

One Rule:
The words are everything

Five Guidelines:

I
Shakespeare wrote what he meant.

II
If it isn't mentioned in the play, it didn't happen, or is not important.

III
Characters never lie to the audience.

IV
The words are tools, not just poetry.

V
Truth beats reality.

The One Rule

Above all else, the words are *everything!*

How they are used, repeated, changed, arranged, pronounced, and unspoken will direct us in all things.

Without exaggeration, the words are everything. When Shakespeare's plays were written, there were no prolonged rehearsals, no director telling actors where to stand. In fact, there were very few stage directions at all. Most of them were added later by editors for clarification or taken from prompt books made by someone other than the author. The only way the actors knew where they were, to whom they were speaking, and when they should enter or exit was by reading the lines.

At the end of Hamlet's "To be, or not to be" monologue (*example a*) he suddenly breaks from his thoughts and says: "Soft you now, / The fair Ophelia!" This tells the actor playing Hamlet that this is the moment when he discovers Ophelia and tells the actor playing Ophelia that if she's wandered offstage during the previous monologue (ignoring her father's direction to stay: "Ophelia, walk you here"), then she needs to hustle back onto the stage.

Example a

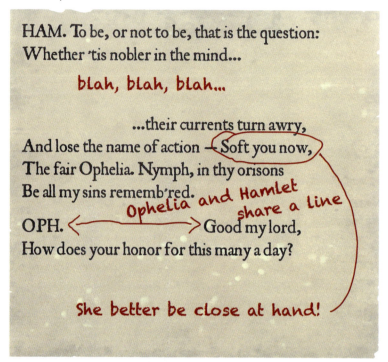

Hamlet, Act III scene 1

There is more than just stage direction in the words. We also learn how characters are feeling, how quickly they are speaking, what social status they hold, and how smart they are (or believe they are). Do they know what they want? Do they know where they are going? The words will tell us. Embedded in the words, we'll hear the rhythm of the play, the very breath and soul of the story.

Example b

In *The Winter's Tale*, Act 1, Scene 2. Leontes's lines tell us everything we need to know: he is jealous, his heart is palpitating, and he is in a severe emotional state. His lines also direct the other actors in the scene to interact in a way that will allow him to mistake their innocent conversation for sexual attraction.

Example b

Hermione gives her hand to Polixenes.

LEON.
Aside. Too hot, too hot!
To mingle friendship far is mingling bloods.
I have tremor cordis on me; my heart dances,
But not for joy; not joy. This entertainment
May a free face put on, derive a liberty
From heartiness, from bounty, fertile bosom,
And well become the agent; 't may—I grant.
But to be paddling palms and pinching fingers,
As now they are, and making practic'd smiles,
As in a looking-glass; and then to sigh, as 'twere
The mort o' th' deer—O, that is entertainment
My bosom likes not, nor my brows!

Guideline I

Shakespeare wrote what he meant.

Are all the plays his, word for word, as he actually set them down? Considering everything these scripts went through, from pen to production, before going into print, it's hard to say yes with absolute certainty. Even taking into consideration the plays he co-authored (Henry VI, Part 1), or contributed only small parts to (Henry VIII, or The Two Noble Kinsmen) still leaves room for asking "Which parts?" And, then again, "Are those parts word for word as he set them down?"

Trouble comes from a few scholars and enthusiasts of Shakespeare, who have called into question the authenticity of his authorship, since 1785. "How could one man write all of this?" they ask, or "How could a man like Shakespeare write any of this?"

While these are fine topics for a healthy debate or enriching discussion, they can distract us from the most important thing: the plays. In practice, or in pursuit of enjoyment, it is important to keep from second-guessing the text. If we question the validity of the words it becomes too easy to alter the language, fitting it to our needs rather than digging deeper to uncover a better understanding of it.

To prevent extraneous nonsense, as we analyze the plays, we need to focus on the essentials that will drive us forward and keep us in the story. By taking it as a given that Shakespeare wrote everything as he intended to, and remembering the one rule, "The words are everything," we give ourselves a solid blueprint from which to work.

Say we decide the text, as written, is infallible. Perfect, we're on our way to Elysium. So what happens when we come across an error or an obvious mistake? Simple: the fault (if it even is one) is not the author's but the character's. This approach forces us to seek answers outside of our own limited experience. If the author makes the mistake, it leads to a correction. But if the character makes the mistake it leads to questions: Why did he or she say that? What did they really mean? Why didn't they know that? Questions, such as these, are important because they keep us invested in the world of the play. It might mean a little more work and a lot of head-scratching, but the results are much more useful and rewarding.

Example 1a

In Act 1, Scene 2 of *The Tempest*, beginning around line 66, Prospero's syntax becomes very choppy and hard to understand. If we see it as a problem in the writing we might be tempted to fix it and change the text to satisfy our own confusion. Yet if we reject such cosmetic choices, and instead choose to deal with the lines as intended, we might be provoked into asking why Prospero's speech is so hard to follow, leading us to the possibility that his emotions are getting the better of him and making clear speech difficult.

Example 1a

PROS. My brother and thy uncle, call'd Antonio —
I pray thee mark me — that a brother should
Be so perfidious! — he whom next thyself
Of all the world I lov'd, and to him put
The manage of my state, as at that time
Through all the signories it was the first,
And Prospero the prime duke, being so reputed
In dignity, and for the liberal arts
Without a parallel; those being all my study,
The government I cast upon my brother,
And to my state grew stranger, being transported
And rapt in secret studies. Thy false uncle —
Dost thou attend me?   *Ah, what?*

Devouring Shakespeare: Five Simple Tools

Stage Directions

While it serves our purposes to grant that Shakespeare wrote all the dialogue as intended, the same cannot be said for stage directions. Shakespeare may have written a few of them (most famous, *"Exit pursued by a bear"*), but most were added later by editors, seeking to clarify the action, or taken from prompt books that simply recorded how things were done in a particular production.

Shakespeare did the majority of his directing in the lines, so the dialogue should always take precedence over the stage directions.

> ***Example 1b***
> In Act 1, Scene 1 of *Romeo and Juliet,* the characters Sampson and Gregory—two servants of the House of Capulet—are trying to pick a fight with Abraham and Balthasar—two servants of the House of Montague. A stage direction reads: Enter Benvolio. The very next line belongs to Gregory, who says: "Say 'better,' here comes one of my master's kinsmen."
>
> This is confusing, because Benvolio is Montague's nephew, not Capulet's. Gregory's line is actually referring to Tybalt, who is a kinsman to Capulet. But the stage directions have Tybalt entering four lines after Gregory says, "Here comes one of my master's kinsmen."

Example 1b

BR. Do you bite your thumb at us, sir?

SAM. I do bite my thumb, sir.

ABR. Do you bite your thumb at us, sir?

SAM. Is the law of our side if I say ay?

GRE. No.

SAM. No, sir, I do not bite my thumb at you, sir, but I bite my thumb, sir.

GRE. Do you quarrel, sir?

ABR. Quarrel, sir? No, sir.

SAM. But if you do, sir, I am for you. I serve as good a man as you.

ABR. No better?

SAM. Well, sir.

(Enter Benvolio.)

GRE. Say "better," here comes one of my master's kinsmen. *Not referring to Benvolio!*

SAM. Yes, better, sir.

> ABR. You lie.
>
> SAM. Draw, if you be men. Gregory, remember thy washing blow.
>
> *(They fight.)* ← Good stage direction.
>
> BEN. Part, fools!
> Put up your swords, you know not what you do.
>
> *(Enter Tybalt.)* ←
>
> TYB. What, art thou drawn among these heartless hinds?
> Turn thee, Benvolio, look upon thy death.
>
> Confusing stage direction. Tyblat is the kinsmen Gregory is speaking of!

This may have been a piece of staging or someone not paying attention . . . and while Benvolio speaks first in this scene, it is clear the line refers to Tybalt.

The lesson? Toss out the stage directions, and let the lines show you the way.

Leave dialogue, change stage directions.

ABR. No better?

SAM. Well, sir.

Enter Tybalt.

GRE. Say "better," here comes one of my master's kinsmen.

SAM. Yes, better, sir.

ABR. You lie.

SAM. Draw, if you be men. Gregory, remember thy washing blow.

They fight.

Enter Benvolio.

BEN. Part, fools!
Put up your swords, you know not what you do.

TYB. What, art thou drawn among these heartless hinds?
Turn thee, Benvolio, look upon thy death.

Guideline II

If it isn't mentioned in the play, it didn't happen or isn't important.

By their very nature, these plays ask more questions than they answer, leaving the audience to ponder a multitude of possibilities—one of the reasons they have endured for centuries. In an environment designed to stimulate the imagination and provoke questions, we run the risk of losing our way by getting hung up on details that don't serve the play.

The main purpose of this guideline is to keep our focus on the ideas and issues Shakespeare actually deals with, thereby keeping us from going off in too many different directions. It can help us clarify the forward-moving action of the play. Shakespeare gives us lots to contend with. There are numerous opportunities to be confounded by thinking *what if*. Which is not to say that what if is detrimental. On the contrary, *what if* is an important part of the creative process—as long as it serves the story. Unchecked, *what if* can distort events within the play and confuse our attempts to understand the basic plot.

> *Example*
> "What if Gertrude orchestrated the death of her husband, old Hamlet? Nothing in the play suggests she did, but then nothing decisively says she didn't, either—unless you consider the fact that Claudius never speaks of the murder with her. A case for such an aberration could be made by a production, cleverly inserting Gertrude as an accomplice into their version. Yet there is nothing in the play, as it stands, that resolves a subplot like that, without some rewrites. Sure, her death could resolve things and bring justice to a wicked Queen, but what about Ophelia? She dies, too—was she in on the plot? Polonius? Horatio? Horatio! Horatio must be the true architect of this whole tragedy, in league with the witches from Macbeth possibly. We may not see them, but surely this is the kind of thing they would do . . . and that means Horatio gets away with it!"

Wild ideas might be fun, especially when we see them attempted on stage, but initially they will not help us understand or make use of the play.

If we accept what the author has given us—and that it is written as intended—then we need to trust that when something isn't mentioned, we can let it go.

Example 2a
Why are the families feuding in *Romeo and Juliet*? It's perfectly acceptable for productions to deal with this background question, especially if it serves some social or moral purpose for the audience. Ultimately, the reason for the feud isn't as important as the violence it produces or the consequences of that violence.

Example 2a

CHORUS.
Two households, both alike in dignity,
In fair Verona, where we lay our scene,
From ancient grudge break to new mutiny,
Where civil blood makes civil hands unclean.
From forth the fatal loins of these two foes
A pair of star-cross'd lovers take their life;
Whose misadventur'd piteous overthrows
Doth with their death bury their parents' strife.
The fearful passage of their death-mark'd love,
And the continuance of their parents' rage,
Which, but their children's end, nought could remove,
Is now the two hours' traffic of our stage;
The which if you with patient ears attend,
What here shall miss, our toil shall strive to mend.

There are instances in Shakespeare where results appear to be more important than the reasons behind them. The provided justification or cause is so slight that it barely registers as adequate motivation. Take Iago's weak reason for hating Othello (*example 2b*).

If Shakespeare chooses not to emphasize something, chances are it's not crucial to understanding the play. In the application of Shakespeare, however, it is up to each production team, actor, reader, or audience member to decide how best to deal with these gaps. Once all of the crucial questions of the play have been dealt with the rest is a matter of creativity and self-expression. There is no right answer.

Example 2b

IAGO.   ...I hate the Moor,
And it is thought abroad that 'twixt my sheets
H'as done my office. I know not if't be true,
But I, for mere suspicion in that kind,
Will do as if for surety. He holds me well,
The better shall my purpose work on him.

Is this really enough reason to justify the terrible things Iago does throughout the play? There's probably a lot more to it, but it's all we get. Shakespeare has chosen to focus on the result of hate rather than the cause, leaving us to wonder forever.

Guideline III

Characters never lie to the audience.

As eyewitness observers, the audience will always be shown the truth. This is very important. Often our entrance into the world of the play depends on our relationship with a single character. He or she can even address us directly, through asides or soliloquies, relaying crucial information about the story. We need to know we can trust that character.

There are only four things any character can address in a play: another character, themselves, the Gods, or the audience. Only one of these can be lied to. (*Hint*: another character.)

Plenty of lies are told in Shakespeare—but never to the audience. Lies and deceit are for people inside the play. Characters may *try* lying to themselves, but they may as well try lying to the Gods. Either way, the truth cannot be hidden. The same goes for the audience. We always get to see the truth. That's one of the main reasons for theatre in the first place—to reveal truths. While a character may not reveal everything to us, what is revealed will be the truth.

Once a character breaks from the world of the play and talks directly to us, we know they can be trusted. No matter how villainous they behave—like Richard III, Iago, or Macbeth—he or she will not lie to us. In many cases, characters take pride in showing us how well they can lie to their fellow characters. But this only works when we know what the truth is.

> *Example 3a*
> A perfect example of a character who tells the audience the truth while lying to everyone in the play is the Duke of Gloucester (Richard III) at the end of *Henry VI, Part 3*, Act 5, Scene 7.

Even when characters don't speak directly to the audience but have private moments that show us what's going on inside their heads, they do not lie.

For instance, Claudius, in Act 3, Scene 3 of *Hamlet*: The king, in a private moment, struggles with what he has done (*example 3b*), and reveals to us a guilty, but unrepentant, conscience. His dialogue is not meant for any of the characters in the play to hear; rather, he speaks to God, himself, the audience, or a combination of all three. Whichever it may be, we are getting a peek inside his soul. The fact that he is speaking out loud is only a theatrical convention, allowing

Example 3a

> **GLOU.** I'll blast his harvest, and your head were laid,
> For yet I am not look'd on in the world.
> This shoulder was ordain'd so thick to heave,
> And heave it shall some weight, or break my back:
> Work thou the way—and that shall execute. *truth*

K. EDW. Clarence and Gloucester, love my lovely queen, And kiss your princely nephew, brothers both.

CLAR. The duty that I owe unto your Majesty I seal upon the lips of this sweet babe.

Q. ELIZ. Thanks, noble Clarence, worthy brother, thanks.

Lies!

GLOU. And that I love the tree from whence thou sprang'st, Witness the loving kiss I give the fruit.

Aside.

> To say the truth, so Judas kiss'd his master, And cried "All hail!" when as he meant all harm.
>
> *truth*

Richard, Duke of Gloucester, plays nice with the other characters in the scene while showing his true face to the audience.

Devouring Shakespeare: Five Simple Tools

us to follow the story. The words—the author's only tools—are in actuality the character's thoughts and emotions, churning away inside of him.

No matter how many lies he or she tells, any character who opens up to the audience will always show a true self—even if unintentionally.

Example 3b

> KING. O, my offense is rank, it smells to heaven,
> It hath the primal eldest curse upon't,
> A brother's murder. Pray can I not,
> Though inclination be as sharp as will.
> My stronger guilt defeats my strong intent,
> And, like a man to double business bound,
> I stand in pause where I shall first begin,
> And both neglect. What if this cursed hand
> Were thicker than itself with brother's blood,
> Is there not rain enough in the sweet heavens
> To wash it white as snow? Whereto serves mercy
> But to confront the visage of offense?
> And what's in prayer but this twofold force,
> To be forestalled ere we come to fall,
> Or pardon'd being down? then I'll look up.
> My fault is past, but, O, what form of prayer
> Can serve my turn? "Forgive me my foul murder"?
> That cannot be, since I am still possess'd

Of those effects for which I did the murder:
My crown, mine own ambition, and my queen.
May one be pardon'd and retain th' offense?
In the corrupted currents of this world
Offense's gilded hand may shove by justice,
And oft 'tis seen the wicked prize itself
Buys out the law, but 'tis not so above:
There is no shuffling, there the action lies
In his true nature, and we ourselves compell'd,
Even to the teeth and forehead of our faults,
To give in evidence. What then? What rests?
Try what repentance can. What can it not?
Yet what can it, when one can not repent?
O wretched state! O bosom black as death!
O limed soul, that struggling to be free
Art more engag'd! Help, angels! Make assay,
Bow, stubborn knees, and heart, with strings of steel,
Be soft as sinews of the new-born babe!
All may be well.

Guideline IV

The words are tools, not just poetry.

It is very tempting, when first encountering Shakespeare, to get caught up in the poetry. The melody of his words can be truly sublime, but there is more to them than just sweet, sweet music.

It is a fundamental element of acting, and certainly true in Shakespeare, that every word spoken on stage has some specific purpose. The kinds of words used, the repetition, the rhythm, the breaking of verse are all means to an end. Whether a character is sharing his or her thoughts as inward or outward expression, the words are tools employed for one purpose: to get something.

This is not to say we can ignore the poetry. On the contrary, we need to embrace it as a gauge for measuring a characters passion. The more poetic the language is (whether he's writing in prose or blank verse), the stronger the emotions are going to be. If words are tools, poetry tells us how fiercely to use them.

Example 4a
Act 3, Scene 5 of *Romeo and Juliet*, the scene in which the lovers must part, is emotionally charged. As Romeo descends from Juliet's window, she has nothing but her words with which to reach her departing love. Her choice of words shows just how intense her feelings are. Time is running out and she has no other way to connect with him than through words, so they need to count. She calls Romeo love, lord, husband, and friend. Any one of these would describe him, but at this moment, one alone is not enough. Where they fail individually, they succeed collectively, expressing that he is everything to her.

This guideline is closely tied to our one rule: the words are everything. The words Shakespeare arms his characters with are not only powerful tools but also indications of the job they need to accomplish. If you are handed a shovel, it's a safe bet you are going to be digging. A hammer has many creative uses, but it's not going to be the best tool for sewing a double half-stitch. Speaking the words "Blow, winds, and crack your cheeks! rage, blow!", lets a performer know they are in for some heavy scene work indeed.

While it's difficult to dictate a right way for each tool to be used, it's safe to say that choosing the best tool for a specific job is the best way to achieve dramatic results. If you let them, the words will tell you the task they are meant for.

Example 4a

ROM.
Farewell, farewell! One kiss, and I'll descend.

he climbs down

JUL.
Art thou gone so? Love, lord, ay husband, friend!
I must hear from thee every day in the hour,
For in a minute there are many days.
O, by this count I shall be much in years
Ere I again behold my Romeo!

That's a lot of suffering if he doesn't write.

ROM.
                    Farewell!
I will omit no opportunity
That may convey my greetings, love, to thee.

It worked. He'll write!

At other times, it's the author who uses the tools, giving his characters poetic descriptions to convey specific images. When Shakespeare needs the audience to see something in graphic detail, he uses his words like special effects, immersing us in his world.

Devouring Shakespeare: Five Simple Tools

> **Example 4b**
> In Act 5, Scene 6 of *Henry VI, Part 3*, after Richard, Duke of Gloucester, stabs King Henry VI, the gruesome visuals he paints for the audience are delivered through some very pretty poetic words.

Whatever the purpose, there are very specific conscious and unconscious reasons why characters choose the words they use. Trying to uncover those reasons will give us tremendous insight into the characters. Employing this guideline is a major key in unlocking a play through its language.

Example 4b

K. HEN. ... thou cam'st to bite the world;
And if the rest be true which I have heard,
Thou cam'st—

GLOU. I'll hear no more; die, prophet, in thy speech:

Stabs him.

For this, amongst the rest, was I ordain'd.

K. HEN. Ay, and for much more slaughter after this.
O God forgive my sins, and pardon thee!

Dies.

GLOU. What? will the aspiring blood of Lancaster
Sink in the ground? I thought it would have mounted.
See how my sword weeps for the poor king's death!
O may such purple tears be alway shed
From those that wish the downfall of our house!
If any spark of life be yet remaining,
Down, down to hell, and say I sent thee thither—

Stabs him again.

I, that have neither pity, love, nor fear.

the Kings blood dripping from the weapon!

Purple tears = drops of blood

Devouring Shakespeare: Five Simple Tools

Guideline V

Truth beats reality.

If you have to choose between truth and reality, choose truth. Reality just gets in the way.

Truth versus reality: What's the difference? These concepts can appear to be the same, but they are not. For our purposes here, reality is the state of things as they actually exist, and truth is a state of perception based on fact or belief.

"The sky is blue." This is a true statement. "The sky is beautiful" is also a true statement. But the reality of it is "The sky only looks blue. The color is actually light traveling through transparent solids in the atmosphere causing sky radiation." Understanding reality brings us knowledge, but it's not always the best way to express how we feel.

Reality is we're watching a play filled with actors pretending to be people to tell us a story. There's no getting away from that fact. As lost in the moment as we might become, we're always going to be aware of where we are and what we're doing. Reality can be suspended, however. For any play, movie, or story to work, reality must be set aside so that we can become immersed in its truth.

Trying to bring too much reality—as we've defined it—into Shakespeare only points out how unreal the world of Shakespeare is. The characters in his plays speak in poetry; they live in a world designed to have few props and no realistic sets, often dependant on the audience's imagination. It isn't necessary to impose outside realism into Shakespeare, because the truth of his plays will create their own reality. The plays exist in a dreamlike, slightly ambiguous time and place and are more concerned with the life and spirit of humanity than anything else.

For Shakespeare and his audience, reality was not as important as the story and the capacity to entertain and be entertained. Costumes were not historically accurate: at most, a character or two might have worn some period accessory, such as a pair of medieval shoes or a toga, but only for flavor. In fact, there weren't really any costumes, as we understand them today. Actors wore modern clothing (hand-me-downs from the theatre troupe's noble patron), which were more about making a good impression than about transporting anyone to the correct time period.

Throughout Shakespeare, you'll find examples of characters knowing things they shouldn't, making journeys in impossibly short amounts of time, and sailing into seaports of cities that are nowhere near the sea. Time and place are insignificant when the plot needs to move forward. When

Lady Capulet knows where Romeo lives in Mantua, even though he left only five minutes before; when Hamlet meets the ghost of his father at midnight, the sun rising just ten minutes later; when Cleopatra has a clock and plays billiards—these are not accurate in reality, but true in Shakespeare.

We live in reality every day. It isn't going to disappear if we spend a couple hours absorbed in a play. Suspend disbelief, and let the truth of the words work within you.

Example 5a

> TREB. There is no fear in him; let him not die,
> For he will live, and laugh at this hereafter.
>
> *(Clock strikes.)*
>
> BRU. Peace, count the clock.
>
> CAS.   The clock hath stricken three.
>
> TREB. 'Tis time to part.

No clocks in the time of Julius Caesar!

Not the point!

Julius Caesar Act II, scene 1

Conclusion

"To business that we love we rise betime
And go to't with delight."
— *Antony and Cleopatra* 4.4, Antony

I hope you found this guide useful. At the very least, it offers an excellent place to start by providing a familiar set of reference points to turn to. Every time I venture into a play by Shakespeare, I start off by trying to forget some of what I know in hopes that I can see it clearly again, scrubbing away hundreds of years of opinion and analysis, looking for the story in its barest form. Like any other craftsman creating, dismantling, or repairing, I would be foolish to attempt the task without the right tools.

May these guidelines serve you as well as they continue to serve me.

Time Line

For one reason or another, I'm always looking for a chronological list of the plays. By putting one in my own book, I'd always know where to find it. The following information may vary depending on the source but is close enough according to Stanley Wells and Gary Taylor's *Complete Oxford Shakespeare*—as represented in *Shakespeare's Words: A Glossary and Language Companion,* by David Crystal and Ben Crystal.

The Two Gentlemen of Verona	1589-1593
The Taming of the Shrew	1590-1593
Edward III	1590-1594
Henry VI part 3	1590-1592
Henry VI part 2	1590-1591
Titus Andronicus	1590-1591
Henry VI part 1	1591-1592
Richard III	1592-1592
The Comedy of Errors	1592-1594
Love's Labor's Lost	1593-1595
A Midsummer Night's Dream	1594-1595
Romeo & Juliet	1594-1595
Richard II	1594-1596
King John	1594-1596
The Merchant of Venice	1596-1597

Henry IV part 1	1596-1597
The Merry Wives of Windsor	1597
Henry IV part 2	1597-1598
Much Ado about Nothing	1598-1599
Henry V	1599
Julius Caesar	1599
As You Like It	1599-1600
Hamlet	1600-1601
Twelfth Night	1601-1602
Troilus & Cressida	1602-1603
Measure for Measure	1604
Othello	1603-1604
All's Well That End's Well	1603-1605
Timon of Athens	1604-1607
King Lear	1605-1608
Macbeth	1606
Antony & Cleopatra	1606-1607
Pericles	1608-1609
Coriolanus	1608
The Winter's Tale	1609-1610
Cymbeline	1610-1611
The Tempest	1610-1611
Henry VIII	1613
The Two Noble Kinsmen	1613-1615

References

It would be very difficult, if not impossible, to single out the specific sources that led to this guide. The ideas expressed here come from many years of experience with Shakespeare and theatre in general. On the other hand, it's very easy to look at my bookshelf and pick out a few of the books I've found to be invaluable resources, the ones that not only match my own views of Shakespeare and theatre, but also continue to expand them.

Ball, David
Backwards & Forwards. A technical Manual for reading plays
Southern Illinois University, 1983.

Brockett, Oscar G
Historical Edition. The Theatre: an introduction
New York: Holt, Rinehart and Winston, 1979.

Brook, Peter
The Empty Space
New York: Atheneum, 1968.

Crystal, David and Crystal, Ben
Shakespeare's Words
A Glossary and Language Companion.
New York: Penguin Group, 2002.

Epstein, Norrie
The Friendly Shakespeare
New York: Penguin Group, 1993.

Garber, Marjorie B
Shakespeare After All
New York: Anchor Books, 2005.

Hattaway, Michael
The Cambridge Companion to Shakespeare's History Plays
Cambridge: The Press Syndicate of the Univ. of Cambridge, 2002.

Kastan, David Scott
Shakespeare after Theory
New York: Routledge, 1999.

Kott, John
Shakespeare our Contemporary
New York: W.W. Norton & Company, 1964.

Onions, C.T.
A Shakespeare Glossary
New York: Oxford University Press, 1986.

Secara, Maggie
A Compendium of Common Knowledge 1558-1603: Elizabethan Commonplaces for writers, Actors & Re-enactors
Los Angeles, CA: Popinjay Pres, 2008

The Oxford Universal Dictionary. Third Edition.
London: Oxford University Press, 1955

Notes

Notes

About the author

Ehren Ziegler studied at the U.S. International University, in San Diego CA., and the National Shakespeare Conservatory in New York. He currently hosts Chop Bard, the podcast he started in 2008.

www.inyourearshakespeare.com

Made in the USA
Lexington, KY
10 December 2011